The Alphabet

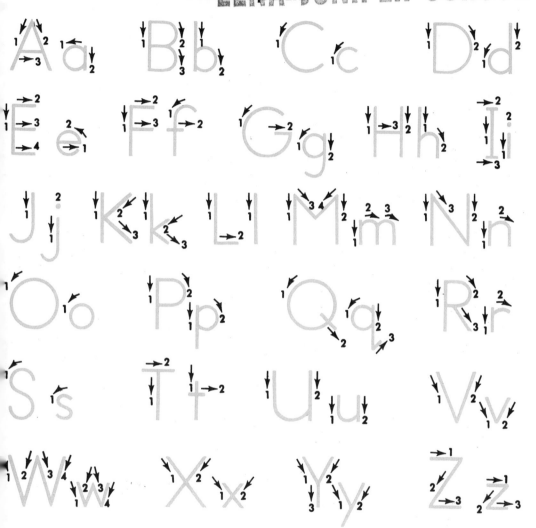

Numerals

MY LITTLE PICTIONARY

OF WORDS I KNOW
OR WANT TO KNOW

animal
bear
bee
bird

frog

Marion Monroe

W. Cabell Greet

SCOTT, FORESMAN AND COMPANY
ATLANTA DALLAS GLENVIEW PALO ALTO OAKLAND, N. J.

CONTENTS

Words for People

aunt	girl	neighbor
babies	grandfather	people
baby	grandmother	principal
boy	he	she
brother	her	sister
child	herself	son
children	him	them
class	himself	they
classes	I	uncle
council	man	us
cousin	me	we
dad	men	who
daughter	Miss	woman
everybody	mom	women
families	mother	workman
family	Mr.	workmen
father	Mrs.	you
friend	myself	yourself

Words for People

clown

painter

twins

farmer

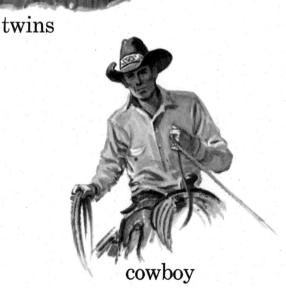

cowboy

Words for People

barber

dentist

nurse

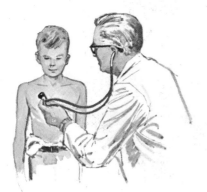

doctor

teacher

Words for People

policeman

mailman

postman

milkman

salesman

fireman

Words for People

checker

clerk

elevator operator

typist

waitress

10

Words for People

pilot

astronaut

plumber

mechanic

truck driver

Words for Storybook People

king   queen

prince   princess

knight

Words for Storybook People

elf

fairy

witch

ghost

giant

Santa Claus

13

Words for Animals

animal	fish	mouse
ant	fishes	owl
bear	flies	pet
bee	fly	pig
bird	fox	ponies
bluebird	foxes	pony
bug	geese	puppies
bunnies	goat	puppy
bunny	goose	rabbit
calf	hen	rat
calves	horse	robin
cat	insect	rooster
chicken	it	sheep
colt	itself	squirrel
cow	kitten	swan
crow	lamb	them
dog	mammal	they
duck	mice	turkey

Words for Animals

frog

turtle

goldfish

canary

woodpecker

parakeet

snake

caterpillar

worm

15

Words for Animals

raccoon

deer

seal

skunk

beaver

Words for Animals

kangaroo

monkey

penguin

panda

dinosaur

Words for Animals

tiger

camel

lion

rhinoceros

elephant

Words for Animals

zebra

giraffe

alligator

hippopotamus

Words for What We Do and Did

add   added

answer   answered

ask   asked

bake   baked

bang   banged

bark   barked

bathe   bathed

begin   began

bite   bit

bless   blessed

blow   blew

bring   brought

build   built

bump   bumped

burn   burned

buy   bought

buzz   buzzed

call   called

care   cared

change   changed

climb   climbed

come   came

cook   cooked

count   counted

cover   covered

cry   cried

cut   cut

dig   dug

divide   divided

do   did

draw   drew

dress   dressed

drink   drank

drop   dropped

dry   dried

eat   ate

Words for What We Do and Did

fall   fell

feed   fed

feel   felt

fill   filled

find   found

fish   fished

fit   fitted

fix   fixed

fly   flew

force   forced

forget   forgot

frown   frowned

gallop   galloped

get   got

give   gave

go   went

grow   grew

guess   guessed

handle   handled

happen   happened

have   had

hear   heard

heat   heated

help   helped

hide   hid

hit   hit

hold   held

hop   hopped

hope   hoped

hurry   hurried

hurt   hurt

join   joined

jump   jumped

keep   kept

know   knew

laugh   laughed

Words for What We Do and Did

lay   laid

learn   learned

leave   left

let   let

lie   lay

light   lighted

light   lit

like   liked

listen   listened

live   lived

look   looked

lose   lost

love   loved

make   made

march   marched

mark   marked

mean   meant

meet   met

miss   missed

mix   mixed

move   moved

name   named

need   needed

open   opened

own   owned

paint   painted

pay   paid

pick   picked

plant   planted

play   played

please   pleased

point   pointed

pop   popped

prepare   prepared

pretend   pretended

protect   protected

Words for What We Do and Did

puff puffed

pull pulled

push pushed

put put

quarrel quarreled

raise raised

read read

remember remembered

ride rode

ring rang

rise rose

roll rolled

run ran

say said

scare scared

see saw

sell sold

send sent

set set

shake shook

shop shopped

shout shouted

show showed

sing sang

sit sat

sleep slept

smell smelled

smile smiled

speak spoke

splash splashed

squawk squawked

squeal squealed

stamp stamped

start started

stay stayed

step stepped

Words for What We Do and Did

stop   stopped

subtract   subtracted

suppose   supposed

surprise   surprised

swim   swam

swish   swished

take   took

talk   talked

teach   taught

tell   told

test   tested

thank   thanked

think   thought

toot   tooted

touch   touched

train   trained

trick   tricked

trip   tripped

try   tried

turn   turned

use   used

visit   visited

wait   waited

wake   waked

walk   walked

want   wanted

wash   washed

watch   watched

wear   wore

weigh   weighed

whistle   whistled

wish   wished

wonder   wondered

work   worked

worship   worshiped

write   wrote

Words for What We Do and Did

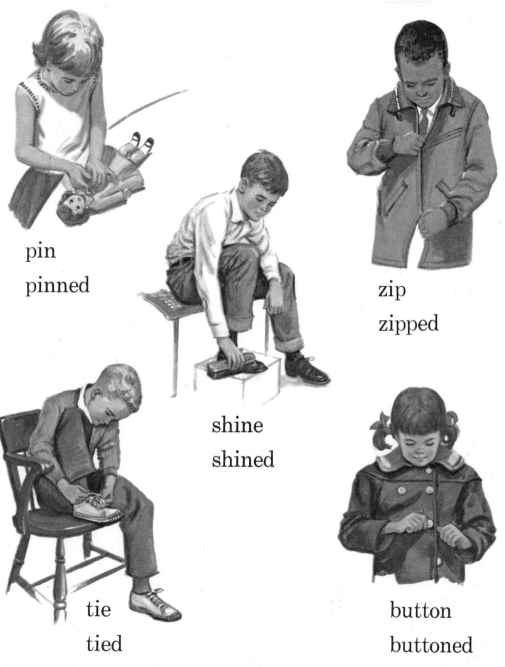

pin
pinned

zip
zipped

shine
shined

tie
tied

button
buttoned

Words for What We Do and Did

crawl
crawled

bend
bent

dance
danced

skip
skipped

leap
leaped

26

Words for What We Do and Did

kick
kicked

bat
batted

carry
carried

throw
threw

catch
caught

Words for What We Do and Did

bounce
bounced

dive
dived

skate
skated

ski
skied

bowl
bowled

28

Words for What We Do and Did

swing
swung

chin
chinned

hang
hung

slide
slid

balance
balanced

29

Words for Things

address

air

axle

ball

bark

basket

bath

beauty

bed

bell

block

boat

book

box

boxes

breakfast

brick

bulb

cake

can

candle

cap

car

cart

cavities

cavity

celebration

chain

chair

clothes

coat

cone

cookie

corn

cover

crib

cup

day

dime

dinner

dollar

door

drink

egg

fence

fire

food

force

fruit

fun

game

gate

ground

handle

Words for Things

hat	merry-go-round	path
heat	minute	pen
hook	mistake	pennies
hour	money	penny
ice	month	picture
it	music	pie
jeans	name	plane
letter	nest	pocket
line	newspaper	point
list	nickel	prize
lunch	noise	problem
lunches	number	pulley
machine	numeral	quarrel
mail	nut	quarter
map	pan	question
mark	paper	race
meat	parties	rain
meeting	party	reason

Words for Things

riddle	stick	truck
root	stone	umbrella
rule	stories	van
secret	story	wagon
seed	sun	water
segment	supper	way
shelf	tail	weather
side	teeth	week
sidewalk	thing	well
sky	tire	wheel
smell	tool	whistle
snow	toot	wind
social	tooth	window
something	top	wing
sound	toy	wood
spot	train	word
stamp	tree	yard
stem	trip	year

Words for Things

apple

bananas

pear

orange

tomato

beans

beets

peas

lettuce

carrots

potatoes

Words for Things

bread

toast

butter

cereal

pizza

popcorn

sandwich

ice cream

candy

soup

Words for Things

chocolate milk

hamburger

orange juice

hot dog

lemonade

milk

peanut butter

jelly

35

Words for Things

belt

pants
slacks

suit

tie

shirt

socks

raincoat

boots

jacket

mittens

Words for Things

scarf

blouse

purse

dress

shoes

gloves

skirt

handkerchief

sweater

bathing suit

pajamas

Words for Things

puzzle

puppet

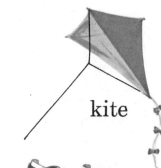

kite

skates

balloon

flashlight

jacks

drum

bicycle
bike

jump rope

doll

38

Words for Things

chalkboard

crayons

chalk

eraser

pencil

scissors

paste

bulletin board

flag

Words for Things

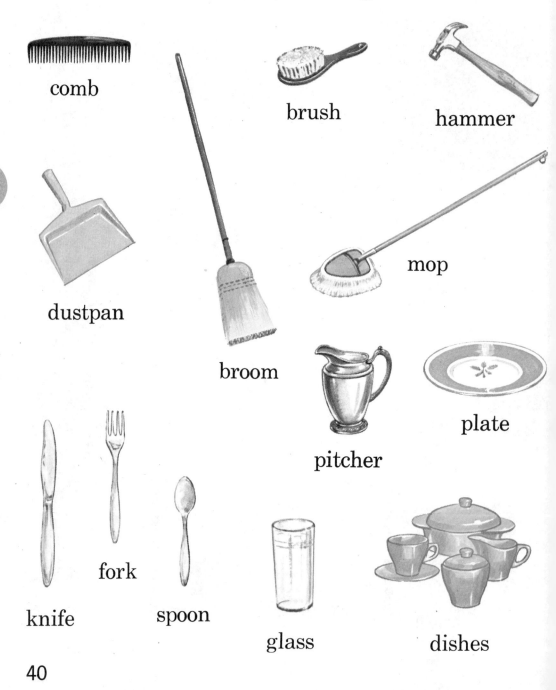

comb

brush

hammer

dustpan

mop

broom

pitcher

plate

knife

fork

spoon

glass

dishes

40

Words for Things

washer and dryer

iron

sink

stool

ironing board

vacuum cleaner

bathtub   refrigerator   stove

Words for Things

radio

sewing machine

toaster

clock

electric fan

telephone

typewriter

record player

Words for Things

desk

plant

lamp

pillow

shelf
shelves

table

piano

television
TV

43

Words for Things

grass

leaf
leaves

flowers

traffic light

mail box

fire hydrant

stop sign

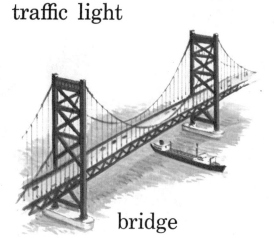

bridge

building

44

Words for Things

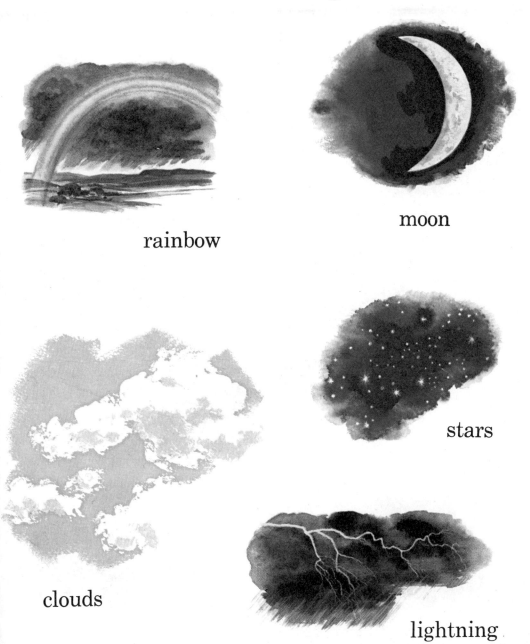

rainbow

moon

clouds

stars

lightning

Words for Things

elevator

jet plane

ship

bus

escalator

taxi

Words for Things

freight train

tractor

street cleaner

power shovel

fire truck

Words for Things

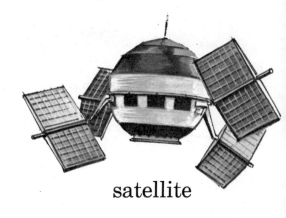

satellite

launching pad

rocket

capsule

48

Words for Things

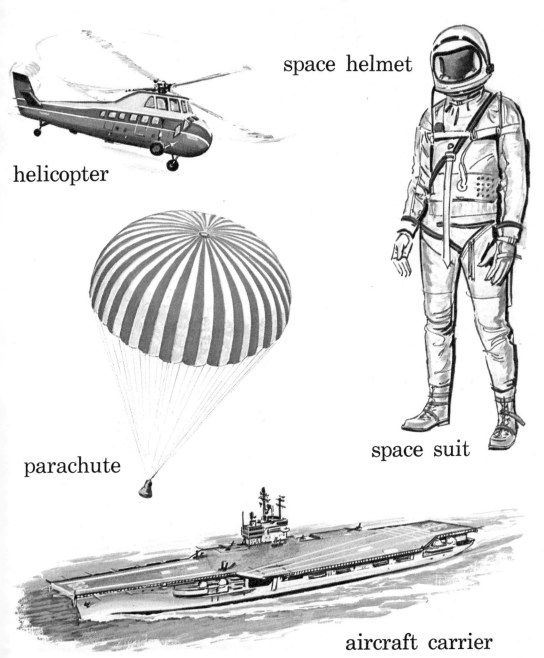

space helmet

helicopter

parachute

space suit

aircraft carrier

Words for Parts of the Body

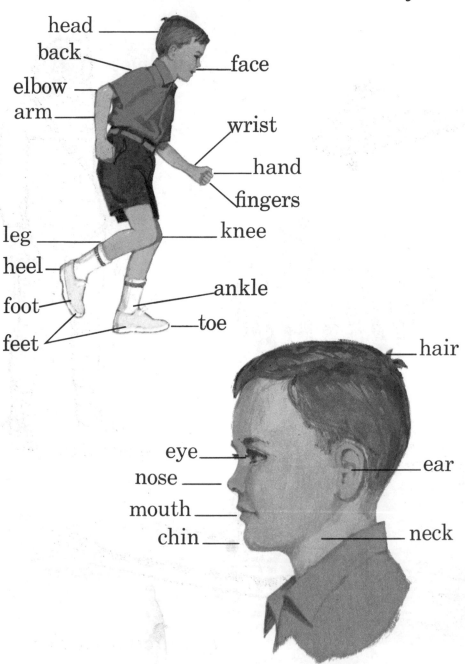

head

back

elbow

arm

face

wrist

hand

fingers

leg

knee

heel

foot

ankle

feet

toe

hair

eye

nose

mouth

chin

ear

neck

Words for Places

America	farm	playground
apartment	field	pond
barn	garden	ranch
beach	hall	ranches
beaches	highway	road
capital	hill	room
church	home	school
churches	house	shop
cities	kitchen	shopping center
city	lake	store
countries	lot	street
country	neighborhood	town
earth	ocean	woods
factories	park	yard
factory	place	zoo

Words for Places

post office

firehouse

theater

aquarium

hospital

Words for Places

library

observatory

supermarket

museum

airport

Words That Tell What Kind

afraid	cloudy	gayer
alike	cold	gayest
asleep	correct	glad
bad	dark	good
beautiful	dear	grassy
more beautiful	deep	great
most beautiful	different	happy
best	dirty	hard
better	dry	helpful
big	easy	high
bigger	fair	hot
biggest	fancy	hungry
busier	fast	ice
busiest	fat	iced
busy	fine	icy
capital	flat	important
clean	funny	interesting
clear	gay	jet

Words That Tell What Kind

jolly	paper	smaller
kind	plaid	smallest
lame	pretty	soft
large	quick	sorry
larger	quiet	still
largest	ready	sudden
left	right	sunny
little	round	sure
long	sad	tall
lost	safe	tiny
low	same	tired
mean	sandy	warm
merry	secret	wee
metal	short	windy
neat	silly	wise
new	sleepy	wonderful
nice	slow	wood
old	small	wrong

Words That Tell What Color

black

orange

blue

pink

brown

purple

gray

red

green

white

lavender

yellow

56

Words That Tell How Much, How Many, or Which One

a   an

about

a little

all

almost

a lot

another

any

as much as

both

cent

dime

dollar

drop

each

else

enough

equal to

every

feet

foot

full

greater than

group

half

hers

his

in all

inch

inches

its

just

last

left

less

less than

long

lots

main

many

mine

more

more than

most

much

my

nickel

no

nothing

number

Words That Tell How Much, How Many, or Which One

only	quarter	this
other	size	those
our	some	value
ours	that	very
own	the	whose
pair	their	yard
pint	theirs	your
quart	these	yours

0 zero

1 one
first

2 two
second

3 three
third

4 four
fourth

5 five
fifth

6 six
sixth

7 seven
seventh

8 eight
eighth

9 nine
ninth

10 ten
tenth

100 hundred

Words That Help Tell Where

above	from	outside
across	front	over
after	here	past
along	high	place
around	in	point
at	indoors	right
away	inside	side
back	into	south
behind	left	there
beside	low	through
between	middle	to
bottom	near	top
by	next	under
center	north	up
down	off	upon
east	on	west
end	out	where
far	outdoors	wherever

Words That Help Tell When

after	late	soon
afternoon	long	spring
again	minute	suddenly
ago	month	summer
always	morning	then
before	near	till
between	never	time
birthday	next	today
by	night	tomorrow
day	noon	tonight
early	now	until
end	o'clock	week
ever	often	when
fall	once	while
from	past	winter
hour	ready	year
in	season	yesterday
last	second	yet

Words That Help Tell When

Sunday	Sun.
Monday	Mon.
Tuesday	Tues.
Wednesday	Wed.
Thursday	Thurs.
Friday	Fri.
Saturday	Sat.

January	Jan.	July	July
February	Feb.	August	Aug.
March	Mar.	September	Sept.
April	Apr.	October	Oct.
May	May	November	Nov.
June	June	December	Dec.

Words That Help Tell When

Hanukkah

Halloween

Flag Day

Christmas

Arbor Day

Columbus Day

Words That Help Tell When

New Year's Day

Thanksgiving Day

Fourth of July

Valentine's Day

Lincoln's Birthday

Washington's Birthday

Little Words That Help

a an	dear	hello
about	didn't	he's
after	does	how
am	doesn't	if
and	done	I'll
any	don't	I'm
are	down	in
aren't	for	into
as	from	is
at	gone	isn't
be	good	it's
because	good-by	I've
been	had	just
but	hadn't	let
can	has	let's
can't	hasn't	like
could	have	may
couldn't	haven't	maybe

Little Words That Help

might	shouldn't	we're
minus	so	weren't
must	such	what
no	than	when
not	thank you	where
of	the	which
off	there	who
oh	they're	who's
on	to	why
only	together	will
or	too	with
over	until	without
perhaps	up	won't
please	upon	would
plus	very	wouldn't
seen	was	yes
she's	wasn't	you'll
should	were	you're

CHILDREN AND WORDS

When children are beginning to read, they first feel the fascination of the complete word, spoken and printed. It is the same fascination that ensnares an adult to spend a half hour reading a dictionary when he had only intended to look up a spelling. He is "out of this world" and into the world of words—their looks, their meanings, their relations with one another, their adaptability to an orderly arrangement where one can count on finding them again. The experience is tonic because it is a reassuring, appetizing exercise in our ways of thought, the logic of our language and culture.

My Little Pictionary is a wordbook, designed to give a child the same sort of experience that adults feel in the dictionary world of words. It encourages the child to write and read independently and to think. It helps make a man of him.

In a child's book of words, pictures are essential for meanings and for appropriate generalizations. Children lack qualifying words and experience, and their thought is intimately related to motion—to "going" and "pretending." Among childhood's favorite games are "going" like the car, the train, the airplane, the cow, or the cat; "pretending" to be the mother, the sheriff, the bad guy, the milkman, Goldilocks, or a roaring lion. Make-believe requires action and words, and often noise. The illustrations in this little book, you will notice, are full of motion: the princess smiles, the beaver gnaws, the snake wriggles, *balance* is a child walking a narrow board. An object named and seen and acted is threefold possessed by the young reader.

The classifications in which the words are grouped in the book are the natural ones a child uses. Wonderfully reassuring to a grammarian is that these classifications are, in effect, the parts of speech. Words for people and things are nouns; words for doing are verbs; words that tell what kind or color are adjectives; words that help tell where and when are adverbial. Words that are less readily defined by or for young children are called, in a plain statement of their function, "Little Words That Help."

It is a good label for them. They are *helpers,* words that help the speaker or writer express himself accurately or vividly. Their specific functions can be more narrowly described later on.

It is important to observe that though points of view in the study of language change, from vocabulary and meaning to function and analysis, the old parts of speech remain substantially the same. They are working parts of the mechanism of our thought and expression.

The arrangement of *My Little Pictionary* was first conceived as a convenient way of making the contents accessible to young children to meet their needs in spelling and written expression. That it does, and much more. You will notice that the classifications of words by meaning in this book are classifications by function, requiring a child to ask himself what any given word is to do in the sentence he is writing. Seeing relationships is implied in that question. If the phrases "words for people and things" and "words for what we do and did" will lead to better understanding of the relationships of words—of syntax—let us adopt them as long as they are useful. The word *syntax* itself was a common Greek noun meaning "a putting together in order, arranging, especially of troops." As soon as a child speaks, he is making use of syntax. If instead of *syntax* we say "How words work together," we will find that a youngster understands, and he in turn may contribute to a discussion of English words and their ways.

I hope that children trained from the threshold of literacy to make these unpretentious classifications of words will later face grammar with equanimity, for equanimity is what one needs to command the structure of one's language. Here in this book are the working parts of speech. They lead directly to the patterns of the language and to a comfortable though analytical knowledge of English uninhibited by hard terms. There is a natural, inevitable grammar of our language, and I believe that this little book points a natural way to it.

W Cabell Greet

SHOWING CHILDREN
HOW TO FIND WORDS

My Little Pictionary is in some ways like a picture book, in other ways like a dictionary—hence its hybrid name. It is designed primarily as a source book of words for children who are learning to read and write. Though such children have had only limited experience with printed language, they are intellectually competent to think about special functions of words in the communication of meaning.

In this book words are grouped in classifications according to their meanings and functions in sentences: words for people, words for things, words for what we do and did, words that tell how many or how much, and so on. The advantages of this organization are plain when one considers the problem of a young child consulting a book in which words are classified alphabetically. Suppose he wants to find the word *eight*. Where is he to look? under the letter *a*, where *ate* may satisfy his idea of the sound of the word? To find a word in *My Little Pictionary*, a child has only to ask himself what the word tells. If he wants to write the word *eight*, he can reason, "I want a word that tells how many," and then turn to that classification. The book helps the child spell correctly, provides him with a means for expressing his ideas in writing, enlarges his reading vocabulary, and encourages him to think about how words work together in sentences.

The book will be most valuable to the child if an adult will take a little time to teach him how to use it. After that, the child can consult the book on his own and look up the spelling of words he wants to use when he writes a letter or a message to a friend, when he makes a list for some purpose, labels a picture to put in a scrapbook, or simply feels an urge to write down something he has just imagined. Although he will not find every word he may need, he can write more independently with *My*

Little Pictionary at hand than he could if he had to ask his teacher or parents to answer his many requests—"How do you spell *princess? giraffe? cried? launching pad?*" Gradually he will also read with greater independence. Words he finds in this reference book and spells correctly as he writes a letter or a little composition will pass into his reading vocabulary. The book itself will also become a source for helping him identify words encountered elsewhere.

When you first give *My Little Pictionary* to the child, allow him to satisfy his curiosity by leafing through the book and discovering that it is full of pictures and words. Then help him find the table of contents on pages 4 and 5. Ask whether he knows what pages like these are for. Be sure he understands that the table of contents will help him find the words he wants in his new book.

Invite the child to read or you read with him the first entry, "Words for People." Ask, "Do you know any words for people?" Accept his replies—perhaps they will be only the names of friends —but add other words, such as *pilot, mailman, doctor, mother, father,* and encourage the child to extend the list.

Call attention to the green half circle in front of the entry "Words for People." Suggest that the youngster find some pages in the book that have the same green half circles on their edges. When these are found, ask what kind of pictures are on the pages and be sure the child understands that all the pictures are of people. Say, "Let's look at the words that are printed on page 6. Can you read some of these words? Are *mother, father, I, you* words for people? Let's look at another page that has a green half circle along the margin. What is this man called who fixes teeth? Yes, he is a dentist, and this word is *dentist.* Can you read the other words for people on this page? Most first-graders will recognize such words as *barber, nurse, teacher* from the pictures. If a child should call the barber a *hair cutter,* give him the correct word. Keep reminding him that on every page marked on the margin with a green half circle all the words are words for people.

Follow the same method with other entries, always going from the table of contents, with its color clue for each classification, to the body of the book. The ability to locate needed entries is

69

an important skill in using any reference book, so give the child time to explore all the classifications. The overview of the book may well take several sittings.

In any source book such as *My Little Pictionary* there must be a range of words that will not overwhelm the beginner and yet satisfy the more advanced child. So all children cannot be expected to read all the words in the printed word lists. Most first-graders have learned to read only some of them, since all words in the basic reading and spelling vocabularies in The New Basic Reading and Language Programs for Grade One and the first half of Grade Two are included, as well as those in the books used in other curriculum areas for these same levels.

If you are introducing a first-grade child to *My Little Pictionary,* tell him that he is getting along fine if he can recognize some of the words in each of the lists. You will notice that each list is alphabetized. Though it is unnecessary to call this arrangement to the child's attention, it allows him to become acquainted with this pattern of organization.

Point out the heading "Words for What We Do and Did," and explain the significance of having the two forms of each word in the list and under each picture. When you talk about the picture section of "Words for What We Do and Did," you may have to explain that in pictures people often look the same whether they are doing the act now or did it yesterday.

When the examination of the book is complete, play a game with the child to see how quickly he can locate a given word.

Question: Listen to this sentence: "The pilot was a young man." Is *pilot* a word for people, animals, or things? Where are the words for people—in the front, the middle, or the back part of *My Little Pictionary?* Where will you find *pilot?*

Answer: I'll find *pilot* near the front of the book under "Words for People."

Continue, asking the child where to find such words as *broom, cake, crawled, hamburger, black, rabbit, zoo, now.* See how rapidly he can not only tell you where to look but locate the word in the book by himself.

For your convenience there is an alphabetized list of all words at the back of *My Little Pictionary*. When a child asks whether or not a certain word is in the book, you can consult this index.

No simple reference book for young children can embrace all the words that creative and well-informed youngsters will want to spell. Each child can supplement this book with an addendum made from a booklet or scrapbook. As a child begins to ask for the spelling of words not in *My Little Pictionary*, encourage him to write these words in his own booklet under similar headings and with the same color clues.

In his own book a budding scientist may write *electronic engineer* under "Words for People." If he is making a collection of rocks, he may write *granite* and *sandstone* under a new heading "Words for Rocks." He may write *turquoise* and *ocher* under "Words That Tell What Color" if *blue, yellow,* and *brown* do not satisfy his sense of exact description. The book he makes may become quite a volume as he pastes into it pictures of unusual interest that he finds in periodicals and newspapers. Help him label these pictures so that he can find the spelling of special words he has selected for his own "Pictionary," a book stimulated by his personal needs and expanded by his growing interests.

As soon as he is ready for it, each child will welcome his own copy of *My Second Pictionary*. This book, an advanced step beyond *My Little Pictionary*, includes both a section devoted to words and pictures arranged alphabetically within classifications and a section with the words arranged alphabetically, with printed definitions similar to those in a beginning dictionary.

The skills required to use and enjoy a dictionary are many and complex. They should begin to develop long before a child encounters the kind of dictionary an adult uses. It is with the hope of helping children on their way to the goal of using a real dictionary with understanding and joy that we present these books.

Marion Monroe

INDEX

There are 1341 words in this Index. Words that are pictured are printed in blue. Words printed in black are found in The New Basic Readers, in the Learn to Listen, Speak, and Write *Series, and in the books used in other curriculum areas through the first half of Grade Two; in the Dolch* Basic Sight Vocabulary of 220 Words, *and in the McKee-Fitzgerald* List A: 350 Most Useful Spelling Words.

73

74

76

79

81

82

The Alphabet

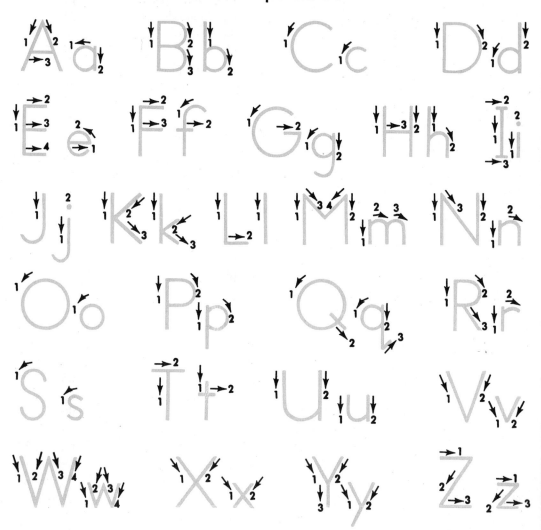

Numerals